MYTHS

BY AGATHA GREGSON

Gareth Stevens
PUBLISHING

Please visit our website, www.garethstevens.com. For a free color catalog of all our high-quality books, call toll free 1-800-542-2595 or fax 1-877-542-2596.

Library of Congress Cataloging-in-Publication Data

Names: Gregson, Agatha, author.
Title: Myths / Agatha Gregson.
Description: New York : Gareth Stevens Publishing, 2020. | Series: Cultures connect us! | Includes index.
Identifiers: LCCN 2018039579| ISBN 9781538238462 (pbk.) | ISBN 9781538238486 (library bound) | ISBN 9781538238479 (6 pack)
Subjects: LCSH: Mythology–Juvenile literature.
Classification: LCC BL304 .G74 2019 | DDC 201/.3–dc23
LC record available at https://lccn.loc.gov/2018039579

Published in 2020 by
Gareth Stevens Publishing
111 East 14th Street, Suite 349
New York, NY 10003

Copyright © 2020 Gareth Stevens Publishing

Designer: Reann Nye
Editor: Therese Shea

Photo credits: series art (background) Lukasz Szwaj/Shutterstock.com; cover, p. 1 Riccardo Botta/EyeEm/Getty Images; p. 5 Triff/Shutterstock.com; p. 7 Maler der Grabkammer der Nefertari/File Upload Bot/Wikimedia Commons; p. 9 IMG Stock Studio/Shutterstock.com; p. 11 ShotgunMavericks/Wikimedia Commons; p. 13 USGS/Avenue/Wikimedia Commons; p. 15 Kiyoweap/Wikimedia Commons; p. 17 Climber 1959/Shutterstock.com; p. 19 Jastrow/Wikimedia Commosn; p. 21 Tyler Olson/Shutterstock.com.

Printed in the United States of America

CPSIA compliance information: Batch #CS19GS: For further information contact Gareth Stevens, New York, New York at 1-800-542-2595.

CONTENTS

A Long, Long Time Ago. 4

Creator Gods. 8

Explaining Natural Events 12

Heroes. 16

Inspiring Stories. 20

Glossary. 22

For More Information. 23

Index 24

Boldface words appear in the glossary.

A Long, Long Time Ago

Today, science has most answers to our questions about nature. But long ago, people knew little about science. They used myths to explain our world. Myths are long-told stories about how and why certain things happened, such as how Earth began.

At first, myths were passed on as stories told aloud. Later, they were written down. Every **culture** has myths because every people wanted to understand the world better. For example, the ancient Egyptians believed the sun god Re created people.

Re

7

Creator Gods

In many cultures, gods and goddesses were the creators of our world. In ancient Greece, Zeus (ZOOS) was the king of the gods. Later, Romans began to tell Greek myths. However, they changed some names and stories. For example, Zeus became Jupiter.

9

A culture's myths and **religions** may be connected. In India, many **Hindus** believe in a power called Brahman. Ancient Hindus honored Brahma, a god who created everything, including good and evil. Brahma was believed to be part of Brahman.

Brahma

11

Explaining Natural Events

In the 1800s, Hawaiians told visitors about the goddesses Pele and Hi'iaka (hee-ee-AH-kah). One day, Pele threw a man into the **volcano** Kilauea (kee-low-AY-ah). To save him, Hi'iaka dug into the volcano. This myth explained Kilauea's shape and **eruptions**.

13

A Japanese myth tells of a giant catfish named Namazu beneath Japan. The god Kashima placed a stone on Namazu's head to keep the fish still. However, sometimes the fish moves—causing **earthquakes**! Today, we know **faults** under Japan cause the earthquakes.

Heroes

Some myths are about amazing people. The Greek hero Heracles, called Hercules by the Romans, had great strength. To make up for a terrible crime, he completed 12 impossible tasks, including killing a monster with nine heads called the Hydra.

Gilgamesh was a hero in the myths of ancient **Mesopotamia**. He looked for a way to live forever. He discovered he couldn't escape death. Gilgamesh may be based on a real king. The myths about him are more than 3,000 years old!

Inspiring Stories

Even though science explains so much now, myths still have a purpose. And they're fun to read! Both Heracles and Gilgamesh **inspired** people to be brave when faced with **challenges** and to accept certain facts of life. What myths inspire you?

GLOSSARY

challenge: a hard problem

culture: the beliefs and ways of life of a group of people

earthquake: a shaking of the ground caused by the movement of Earth's crust

eruption: the bursting forth of hot, liquid rock from within the earth

fault: a break in Earth's crust

Hindu: a follower of a major religion of south Asia

inspire: to cause someone to want to do something

Mesopotamia: the region of Asia between the Tigris and Euphrates Rivers

religion: a belief in and way of honoring a god or gods

volcano: an opening in a planet's surface through which hot, liquid rock sometimes flows

FOR MORE INFORMATION

BOOKS

Ganeri, Anita. *Chinese Myths and Legends*. Chicago, IL: Capstone Raintree, 2013.

Lock, Deborah. *Myths and Legends*. New York, NY: DK Publishing, 2015.

Namm, Diane. *Roman Myths: Retold from the Classic Originals*. New York, NY: Sterling Children's Books, 2014.

WEBSITES

Ancient Gods, Goddesses, and Magical Beings for Kids

ancienthistory.mrdonn.org/gods.html

Discover many more gods, goddesses, and other mythical beings.

5 Terrifying Tales from Greek Mythology

www.natgeokids.com/nz/discover/history/greece/greek-myths/

Read five exciting Greek myths.

INDEX

Brahma 10

Brahman 10

Egyptians 6

Gilgamesh 18, 20

Greek 8, 16

Hawaiians 12

Heracles 16, 20

Hercules 16

Hi'iaka 12

Hindus 10

India 10

Japan 14

Jupiter 8

Kashima 14

Kilauea 12

Mesopotamia 18

Namazu 14

nature 4

Pele 12

Re 6

Romans 8, 16

Zeus 8